Essence of Hinduism
-Basic Doctrines-

- One Supreme Being (every where, in everything)
- Dharma (Righteousness of thought, deed and conduct)
- Respect for all spiritual paths
- Guidance of spiritually awakenend Master
- Trinity (Brahma, Vishnu, Mahesha)
- God incarnates Himself on earth to uphold righteousness
- 'Karma' (Doctrine of cause & effect)
- Divinity of 'Vedas'
- Ahimsa (non-violence)
- 'Moksh' (Freedom from cycle of birth & death)
- Re-incarnation (Cycle of birth & death)

(Courtesy : K. S. Bhalla)

Hindu Temples

Mukteshwar, Bhuneshwar

Birla Mandir, Kolkatta

Somnath, Gujrat

Badrinath, Uttranchal

Gangamandir, Haridwar

Jagannath, Puri (Orissa)

Daksheneshwar, Kolkatta

Meenakashi, Madurai (Tamil Nadu)

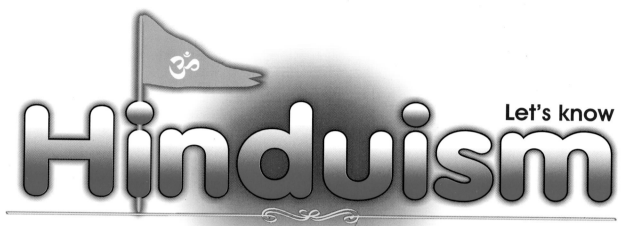

Let's know

Hinduism

The oldest religion of infinite adaptability and diversity

Ramesh Chander Dogra
Urmila Dogra

Dogra, Ramesh and Urmila
Let's know HINDUISM
Star, New Delhi 2003

@Star Publications 2003
ISBN 81-7650-056 9

First Edition : 2003
Price : Rs. 195/-
          (in U.K. £ 8.95)

Published in India by
STAR PUBLICATIONS PVT. LTD.
4/5-B, Asaf Ali Road, New Delhi-110 002
(e-mail: starpub@satyam.net.in)

Distributors in the U.K.:
Star Publishers Distributors
112, Whitfield St., London WIT 5EE (UK)
Tel : 020 - 7 380 0622
E-mail : indbooks@aol.com

Layout & Design
Jupiter Publicity Co.
108, Surya Kiran, K.G. Marg, New Delhi, India
e-mail: wishwell@mantraonline.com

Printed at Swan Press, Naraina, New Delhi

ACKNOWLEDGMENT
The authors are thankful to Consul General K.S. Bhalla,
Mr. Chander Mohan, Ms. Manju Gupta and
Mr. Amarnath Varma for their indepth and valuable
contributions and advice.

CONTENTS

This book is dedicated
to the peace loving people
of all faiths.

Origin of Hinduism

Hinduism is the world's oldest, most tolerant and peace-loving religion. Its origin is traced to the most ancient civilisation of the Indian sub-continent---the Indus civilisation. The valley of River Indus (then known as River Sindhu and from which the term 'Hindus' is derived) was home to more than a hundred settlements as early as over 5,000 years ago. Then followed the early Aryan settlers who possibly entered from the north-west and were responsible for the decline of Indus civilisation. These early Indo-Aryans believed in polytheistic worship of the powers of Nature through prayers, hymns and sacrifice; there was no temple or image worship at that time. Ancient seers and sages through prayers and meditation attained enlightenment and the ultimate experience of God---this constituted the foundation of *Vedic* civilisation. They believed in observance of all the laws and customs called D*harma* or right conduct. A man or woman could remain an orthodox Hindu without even believing in God or theology, or without knowing or reading any sacred book. He/she could honour some convictions from Christianity, Islam, atheism or paganism, but no questions were raised as long as he/she conformed to the *Dharma* (righteousness). It is for this reason that Hinduism is not known just a religion, but a philosophy of life. Thus, Hinduism is not based on any single book or on the words of any single teacher or prophet; it is based on Eternal Truth or righteousness.

Swami Narayan Temple, London (U.K.)

Growth of Hinduism

Hinduism consists of beliefs, practices and socio-religious institutions of the Hindus who are principally the inhabitants of India, Nepal, Sri Lanka and Bali (Indonesia). Large-scale migration of Hindus from India as early as 19th century when they settled in parts of South-east Asia, South Africa, Trinidad, Guyana, Surinam and in islands of Fiji, Mauritius etc. The population of Hindus today is estimated as about 950 millions in various parts of the world, and one in every six persons is supposed to be a Hindu.

The majority of the Hindus migrated to the industrialised countries after the Second World War. They soon established themselves and made a notable contribution to the economic, cultural and social life of their adopted countries.

The history of Hinduism dates back to many thousand years, but Hindus believe that their religion is both a civilisation and a mixture of various religious principles with neither a beginning nor an end. It is a continuous process, even preceding the existence of this earth. As a religion it covers all forms of belief and worship of the divine in every manifestation allowing a Hindu to worship in a church, a mosque or a gurudwara as freely as in a temple. Hinduism is the only religion in the world where it is not essential to go to a temple. It allows absolute freedom of worship---one can meditate on the Divine in one's mind, while being guided by one's own spiritual experiences. Hinduism believes neither in religious guidance nor in observance of

Tableau of Hindu Gods in crowded streets

religious practices. Even an atheist is not excluded from being a Hindu. It is therefore called *Sanatana dharma* (eternal religion or universal righteousness); some call it a fellowship of religions as it has absorbed the faiths of many religions and given birth to many sects.

Hinduism is very complex yet very simple, permeating totally the life of every Hindu from the moment of his/her birth, be he/she a believer or non-believer, a scholar or an illiterate, a meat-eater or a vegetarian. Hinduism is not known as a religion but as a *way of life*. It believes in free thinking and tolerance. All the religions of the world generally have only one book to guide them, but Hinduism has many books which are considered holy, viz., *Vedas, Upanishads, Puranas, Mahabharata, Bhagvad Gita, Ramayana,* etc.

The early Indo-Aryans believed in worship of ancestors who held a place of prominence in their minds and in their social organisation. They prayed for good health and a long life. During Vedic times asceticism was unknown; the family occupied the position of power. Later when the temples were built, everyone was allowed to visit and pray there.

This ancient civilisation of India differs from that of Egypt, Mesopotamia and Greece, as its traditions have been preserved without breaking down of the system till the present day. Romain Rolland (French philosopher, 1886-1944) has said, "If there is one place on the face of the earth where all the dreams of living men have found a home from the very earliest days, it is India."

Birla (Lakshmi Narayan) Temple, New Delhi

Beliefs of Hinduism

Aum/Om is an auspicious and most sacred symbol of Hinduism. It is the divine sound from which life has emerged. It is a combination of letters invested with peculiar sanctity by Hindu mysticism. In the *Vedas* it represents the Trinity (union of three gods---Vishnu, Shiva (called Mahesh also) and Brahma and consciousness; and in the *Puranas*, it is used in the beginning of every sacred act or writing. *Padma Purana* says that the syllable *Aum/Om,* used at the commencement of all prayers, is composed of three letters---'a, u, m'---which are typical of the three *Vedas*. *Om* is said to typify the three spheres of the world---heaven, earth and hell, the three holy fires and the three steps of Vishnu. **Aum/Om** is also a sacred symbol of Hinduism.

**OM,
the auspicious symbol**

Brahma **(the Supreme, all-powerful God):** One of the Gods which Hindus worship is called Brahma, the ultimate reality. Brahma is the supreme soul of the Universe, self-existent, eternal, from which all things emanate, and to which all things return. This Divine essence has no form, is invisible, unborn, uncreated and without a beginning or an end. In other words Brahma is the creator, preserver or transformer and reabsorber of everything. This supreme spirit is often given a form which Hindus call *murti* or image. The One or Whole Brahma has three forms, viz., Brahma (creator), Vishnu (preserver) and Mahesh (destroyer) with their wives Saraswati (goddess of knowledge), Lakshmi (goddess of wealth) and Parvati (the mother goddess) respectively.

Incarnation (*Avtar*): The concept of incarnation is the cornerstone of Hinduism, which believes that God

Brahma, creator of Universe

appears on earth in some form or the other to protect the good and destroy evil. There are supposed to be the following ten incarnations of God:

i. **Matsya (fish):** The object of this incarnation was to save *Vaivaswata,* the seventh *Manu* and progenitor of the human race, from destruction by a deluge.

Matsya Avtar

ii. **Kurma (tortoise):** Vishnu appeared in the form of a tortoise in the *Satya yuga,* the first era, to restore those values which had been lost in the previous deluge. As a tortoise, he placed himself at the bottom of the ocean, and made his back the pivot of mountain called Mandara. The gods and demons twisted a serpent called Vasuk*i* around the mountain, and churned the sea till they recovered the desired nectar (*amrita*) of immorality, Lakshmi (goddess of wealth and beauty), Sura (goddess of wine), Rambha (ideal woman), Parijata (a celestial tree), Ucha (the wonderful horse), Kaustubha (a celebrated jewel), Airavata (a perfect elephant), *shankh* (eternal conch of victory), *dhanush* (a famous bow) and *visha* (the poison).

Kurma Avtar

iii. **Varaha (boar):** A demon, Hiranyaksha, had dragged the earth to the bottom of the sea. To recover it, Vishnu assumed the form of a boar, and after a contest, slew the demon and raised the earth up.

Varah Avtar

iv. **Narasimha (man-lion):** Vishnu assumed this form to save the world from the tyranny of Hiranyakashipu (demon). The demon wanted everyone to worship him, but his son Prahlad worshipped Vishnu. When the demon was about to kill his own son for not worshipping him, Vishnu emerged from the pillar in the incarnation of Narasimha (in the form of half-man and half-lion) and killed the demon to save Prahlad.

Narsimha Avtar

v. **Vaman (dwarf):** In the *Treta yuga,* the demon-king Bali, had by his devotion, acquired domination of the three worlds---heaven, earth and hell, and the demi-gods were shorn of their dignity and power. To amend this, Vishnu took birth as dwarf-son of Kashyapa and Aditi, and appeared before King Bali to beg for alms. The generous King Bali offered as much land as the dwarf could step over in three paces. Vishnu took two steps over heaven and earth each, and then stopped leaving the infernal region to Bali.

Vaman Avtar

Parsuram (6th Avtar)

Rama (7th Avtar)

Krishna (8th Avtar)

Buddha (9th Avtar)

vi. **Parsuram (man with the axe):** Born in *Treta yuga*, as son of the Brahmin Jamadagni, this incarnation saved the *Brahmins* from the arrogant domination of the *Kshatriyas*.

vii. **Rama:** The hero of *Ramayana* and son of King Dasharatha was born to destroy the demon-king Ravana. Rama's bridge (called Adam's bridge in modern maps) is a line of little islands between India and Sri Lanka, which are said to be the remnants of the bridge built by Hanuman's troops to cross over into Sri Lanka to rescue Sita.

viii. **Krishna:** This is the most popular incarnation of Vishnu born to destroy the demon-king, Kansa.

ix. **Buddha:** Vishnu is said to have appeared as Buddha to encourage worship of deities, and discourage belief in demons and the caste system.

x. **Kalki (white horse):** The incarnation of Vishnu is yet to appear at the end of the *Kali yuga*. Seated on a white horse, with a drawn sword blazing like a comet, this incarnation is said to be responsible for the final destruction of the wicked and for restoration of purity.

Punarjanam **(reincarnation):** The mortal soul is continuously born and reborn in one of the 8,400,000 species until it attains liberation.

Moksha or Mukti **(liberation from rebirth):** This is the goal and purpose of life, according to the *Vedanta*. It is the liberation of the soul from the cycle of births and deaths to remain consistently in the service of God. In Hinduism there are many ways to strive for perfection towards *moksha*, with one of them being the worship of God through an image (idol).

Char Dham **(four sacred abodes):** In Hindu belief there are several places known as *tirthas* (pilgrimage centres) visits to which are considered very sacred. But four such *tirthas* are more sacred abodes. These are Badrinath (in Uttaranchal, north India), Puri (in Orissa, east India), Dwarka (in Gujarat, western India), and Rameshwaram (in Tamil Nadu, south India). For devout Hindus the attainment of *moksha* (liberation from the cycle of lives and deaths) is the prime purpose in life and a visit to these four places lead to *moksha* (salvation).

***Guru-shishya parampara* (teacher-disciple relationship):** In the early educational system of India, the *guru* (teacher) received pupils to his own hermitage (*ashram*).

Guru with his disciple

The *shishya* (disciple) gave him unquestioning obedience and reverence. The early system of learning was by word of mouth (oral communication) and was handed down from the *guru* to the *shishya*.

***Dharma* (righteousness):** In its widest sense the word is used to denote the universal laws of Nature that uphold the cosmos. Humans, animals, birds, insects and plants are subject to the laws of Nature. Man's D*harma* changes with time but of others it remains more or less the same. The D*harma* of a human as an infant, a child, youth, adult and an old person changes from one stage to another, but the basic principle of D*harma*---to lead a life of equilibrium in harmony with Nature---remains the same. Similarly, the D*harma* of water is to quench thirst and sustain all forms of life, while the D*harma* of fire is to provide energy and heat. As long as the world and Nature are there, D*harma* will continue to exist.

The term D*harma* also signifies the code of conduct of an individual or a group and these precepts of social behaviour are found in the *Dharma-shastras* (law-scriptures). *Dharma* also means justice, virtue, morality, religious duty, goodness, truth and one's duty performed without expecting any reward.

***Murti puja* (worship of God through idols):** Idolatry did not exist amongst the *Vedic* people. *Jabala Upanishad* says that images (idols) are meant only as aids to meditation and that is why the shape and face of the image changes according to the will of the artist. An image of god or goddess used in worship, can be in the form of a human, animal, plant, or bird or a combination of all. In Hinduism there are many ways to acquire *moksha* (liberation of soul from the cycle of birth), and one of them is by worship of God through an idol.

Worship of Idols

Satya (truth): It is one of the basic virtues in Hindu ethics and the chief pillar of Hindu *dharma*. The earliest of all *yugas* (aeons) was known as *Satya yuga*. Those who speak the Truth without faltering are entitled to a reward and that is a place in *Satya loka* (abode of truth) or Brahma's heaven. In *Mandukya Upanishad* it is mentioned that truth invariably triumphs (*satyameva jayate*); and no wonder, this motto is used on the official crest of Government of India. Even Mahatma Gandhi has entitled his autobiography *My Experiments with Truth*. A person who has invariably spoken the truth can attain the power to make anything come true by simply saying *satyameva jayate*. Manu said that one should speak the truth and pleasantly too. The honesty of Hindus and their love for truth was confirmed by Hieun-Tsang (A.D. 630). Marco Polo (A.D.1293) stated that Hindus are famous for their honesty and would not tell a lie for anything on earth; a British Officer, Sir William Sleeman, who during the 19th century spent his life among the Hindu peasants has said, "I have come across hundreds of cases in which a man's property, liberty and life depended upon his telling a lie, and he refused to tell it."

Ahimsa **(non-violence):** This is another inborn virtue of Hindus, who abhor killing or shedding of blood. Devout Hindus strictly practise abstinence from animal flesh. *Ahimsa* also means living one's life without hurting anyone physically, emotionally, mentally or morally. The doctrine of *ahimsa* is often held up as Hinduism's great contribution to mankind. Mahatma Gandhi carried *ahimsa* from religion to politics and made it popular all over the world.

Buddha: The ninth incarnation

Gau-raksha (cow-protection): Of all the animals, the cow/bull is venerated in Hinduism. The cult of the bull was an integral part of the people living in Indus Valley as is evident from the seal recovered from there. During the Vedic period the bull took a subordinate place to the cow. The cow is regarded in the *Rig Veda* as *aghanya* (not to be slained). In Hindu mythology Kamdhenu and her daughter Surabhi were sacred cows. Lord Krishna is associated with cows and his paradise is called *go-shala* (cowshed). Shiva's bull Nandi is worshipped in Hindu religion. During the *Brahmanical* period in the first century of the present era, cow worship came to occupy a popular place in Hindu religion as it was believed that the cow was created on the same day as Brahma; hence, killing a cow amounted to killing God. By the fourth century, cow killing was made a capital offence during the Gupta period. Even Mahatma Gandhi has said: "Cow-protection is the gift of Hinduism to the world and is one of the most wonderful phenomenon in human evolution. Mother cow is better than the mother who gave us birth. Our mother gives milk for a little while and expects us to serve her when she grows old. Mother cow gives us milk and butter all along and expects from us nothing but grass and grain."

A painting of Radha-Krishna

Doctrine of *Karma*: The doctrine of *karma* and rebirth at a later stage gave character and form to the new system. *Karma* means 'deed or activity' and refers not only to actions undertaken by the body, but also by the mind. *Karma* is in reality actions and reaction of a human beings and Hindus believe that actions produce results in the next birth. The doctrine of *karma* is based upon the following beliefs and assumptions:

● That every act or deed must necessarily be followed by its consequences that are not merely physical but mental and moral in character.

● That the consequences of a person's acts may not be fully experienced in this life but demand consequent births for their fruition or punishment.

● That the inequalities and sufferings in all walks of life are due to the person's deeds in either the present or past life.

● That the doctrine of immortality of the soul justifies the belief in a future existence of the individual and equally justifies its pre-existence as well.

● That happiness or sufferings of a person in this life are due to his *karma* (deeds) in the present or else in the previous birth.

It is believed that a person's *karma* accumulates over the years, with bad deeds increasing the negative side, and good deeds, such as charity, generosity, austerity and asceticism, increasing the positive. In other words, it is believed that only misfortune in this life is the effect of *karma* or one's deeds in the present or previous life. Thus, *karma* was originally a sort of account of credits and debits, a reckoning to be settled at the end of one's life. *Karma* does not create; it only adjusts the effects of good or bad deeds.

Havan : Prayers before the sacred fire

Four stages of life

Vedas give the age of a person as 100 years, and this age has been divided into four equal stages, as given under:

(a) ***Brahmacharya-ashram*** (student life): The student's duty is to pass his days in humble and obedient attendance upon his *guru*/spiritual preceptor in the study of the *Vedas*.

(b) ***Grihasth-ashram*** (married life): The married man lives with his wife as head of a family engaged in performance of the ordinary duties of a householder; reading the *Vedas*; taking part in religious ceremonies; bestowing and receiving alms; and providing assistance for religious ceremonies. According to Manu, a person who has systematically studied the *Vedas* and fully observes the rules of brahmacharya-ashram, is authorised to enter the *grihasth-ashram*.

(c) ***Vanaprasth-ashram*** (the period of retreat from married life): After having discharged his duties as a householder and having led a married life, a man should retire to devote himself to self-denial in food and raiment, to mortification of various kinds, to religious meditation, and to the strict performance of ceremonial duties.

(d) ***Sanyas-ashram*** (renunciation): The religious mendicant, who is free from all forms of duties, wanders about and subsists on alms, practising or striving for that elevated condition of mind where he is heedless of the joys and pains, care and troubles of life and is focused upon the Divine and final absorption.

Buddha mendicants

Four *Yugas* (aeons/eras of the world)

Hinduism has classified the total tenure of the world into four eras and each of these eras is preceded by a period called its *sandhya* (twilight), and is followed by another period of equal length called *sandhyansa* (portion of twilight). The duration of these eras were first computed as under:

(1) **Satya yuga** or **Krita yuga**: This was the age in which righteousness was eternal. There was no malice, sorrow, pride, deceit, hatred, cruelty or fear. Everything was peaceful as in heaven

(2) **Treta yuga**: In this *yuga*, righteousness decreased by one-fourth. People acted with the view to seeking revolts for their rites and rituals, and were no longer disposed towards observing austerity and purity from a simple feeling of duty.

(3) **Dwapara yuga**: In this *yuga*, righteousness diminished by half. A few men studied the *Vedas* and some read none at all. With the decline of goodness, only a few men adhered to Truth with the result that diseases, desires and calamities became a part of their lives.

(4) **Kali yuga**: In this *yuga,* which is prevailing currently, righteousness remains to the extent of one-fourth only. Noble deeds and rites of sacrifice have ceased and replaced with calamities, diseases, fatigue, anger, distress, hunger and fear on the increase. People have been drawn to materialism and consumerism.

The *Satya yuga* or *Krita yuga* lasted for four thousand years; *Treta* for three thousand; *Dwapara* for two thousand; and for *Kali yuga* there is no fixed time.

Goddess Vaishno Devi

15

Worship (Puja) in Hindu Religion

It is well known that, except where devotees assemble for *kirtan* (hymn singing), there is no such thing as congregational worship in Hinduism, as seen in Christianity. Hindu worship is of three kinds. While mental and domestic worship is private and personal, temple worship is performed by priests with the followers of Hinduism.

- **Mental worship**: Any person, be a Hindu or non-Hindu can worship or meditate on God within his mind without visiting a religious place.

- **Domestic worship**: Almost every Hindu household has some sort of a prayer-room decorated with appropriate images or idols or sacred symbols. People sit in front of the idol and read sacred verses (*mantras*) such as *gayatri mantras* or hymns. Flowers are offered with lighted lamps being waved ceremoniously in front of the idol or image.

- **Temple worship**: In almost every Hindu locality, there are temples and shrines. Hinduism is the only religion where it is not essential to go to a temple. Nowadays people visit the temple for purification of soul and for mental peace. Some temples attract very large crowds.

Lord Venkateswara (VISHNU) in South India

Ganesha worship

Ganesha (elephant-God) is considered God of wisdom, good luck, prosperity and remover of obstacles. Hence, he is invariably propitiated at the beginning of any important or auspicious undertaking. He is represented as a short, fat man of yellow colour, with a protuberant belly, four hands, and the head of an elephant sitting on the back of a rat. Each part of this mystical form conveys a message: the elephant head indicates acquisition of knowledge by listening through ears; the tusk symbolizes perfection and imperfection in this world; the trunk stands for physical and mental strength; the large stomach depicts the ability to digest whatever experience life brings; the rat (his vehicle) stands for desire, wealth and remover of obstacles. He has four hands: in one hand he holds an axe and a goad---the axe is to remove obstacles and the goad is to keep his devotees on the path of *dharma* (righteousness). The snare in the other hand symbolises his control over death. In his bottom left hand he holds a sweetmeat, representing a reward for devotion; and with his lower right hand he blesses his devotees.

Legend of Ganesha: There are several legends accounting for Ganesha possessing the face of an elephant. According to one of these legends, one day in the absence of Lord Shiva, his wife Parvati made an image of a boy from the scurf of her body and told her son Ganesha to keep guard while she took her bath. In the meantime, Lord Shiva returned but was stopped by Ganesha to enter, since his mother was bathing. This annoyed Lord Shiva and in a fit of temper, he chopped off Ganesha's head. Later, when Parvati came out and saw the plight of her son, she became extremely agitated. Shiva consoled her by replacing the boy's head with that of an elephant which he saw first. And he further blessed the elephant-faced boy with the gift that all good works and writings would start with his name on the top. Consequently, we invariably find the words *'Shri Ganeshay-namah'* (salute to Ganesha) on the top before any good work is begun.

Ganesha : The Elephant God

Hindu Scriptures

The *Vedas*: The *Vedas* are holy books which constitute the foundation of Hindu religion. They consist of hymns written in an old form of Sanskrit and composed somewhere around 7000 B.C. These were revealed to the *rishis* (sages) whose names they bear. Hence, the whole body of the *Vedas* is known as *sruti* (what is heard). They contain all the wisdom of the Universe: knowledge of art, music, linguistics, literature, economics, religion, weaponry, space science, geometry, logic, technology, hypnotism, mathematics, philosophy, rituals, health, magic, medicine, architecture, aeronautics and spiritual wisdom.

There are four *Vedas*: *Rig Veda*, *Yajur Veda*, *Sama Veda* and *Atharva Veda*. Each *Veda* is divided into two parts: *mantra* and *brahmana*. The *mantras* are instruments of conveying thought involves prayer and praise of the Lord in the metrical hymn. The *brahmana* is a collective term for the treatises and it contains liturgical and ritualistic explanations and applications of the hymns as illustrated by numerous legends.

In the past, young boys and young girls learnt to utter the correct sounds of *Rig Veda* or other *Vedas* by listening to their *guru* or teacher. The hymns were not commonly available in written forms and thus were taught orally. Made to learn the *Vedas* by heart, the students passed on their knowledge acquired orally to the next generation of students.. Now they are available in print in Sanskrit, English and in many other languages of the world.

Puranas: There are eighteen basic *Puranas* which are considered as ancient or old religious literature. Available originally in Sanskrit they describe the exploits of the divinities and cover the following five topics:

- Creation of the Universe.

- Destruction and revival of the Universe.

- Genealogy of the Gods and patriarch, presenting the growth of Hinduism.

- Reign of Manu, whose period is called *Manwantara*.

- History of solar and lunar race of the kings.

ओम् भूर्भुव: स्व:। तत्सवितुर्वरेण्यं
भर्गो देवस्य धीमहि। धियो यो न: प्रचोदयात्।

Om bhur bhuvah swah. Tatsavitur varenayam bhargo devasya dhi mahi. Dhiyo yo nah pracho-dayat.
Oh God, the giver of life, remover of pains and sorrows, bestower of happiness and creator of the Universe, thou art most luminous, pure and adorable. We mediate on thee, may thou inspire and guide our intellect in right direction.

Gayatri Mantra (divine hymns)

Shastras: There are six *shastras* which are the most ancient scriptures of Hinduism:

* *Sankhya shastra* by Maharishi Kapil,
* *Yoga shastra* by Maharishi Patanjali,
* *Nyaya shastra* by Maharishi Gautam,
* *Vaisheshik shastra* by Maharishi Kannad,
* *Purvmimansa shastra* by Maharishi Jemini
* *Vedant shastra* by Mahrishi Vyas.

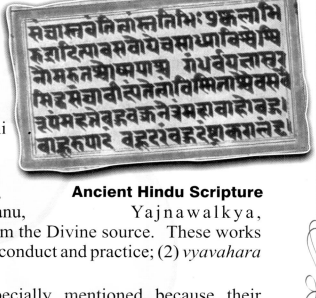

Ancient Hindu Scripture

Dharma-shastra (law book or code of laws): This term includes the entire body of Hindu law, though it comprises basically the laws of Manu, Yajnawalkya, and other inspired sages had received them from the Divine source. These works are divided into three parts: (I) *achar* or rules of conduct and practice; (2) *vyavahara* or judicature; (3) *drayaschitta* or penance.

Manu and *Yajnavalkya* (the sages) are specially mentioned because their contributions were more noteworthy than those of other sages. These two were followed by eighteen other inspired sages who are recognised as authorities on law, and the works ascribed to them are still extant. The writings of these law enunciators have appeared in different forms.

Manu-smriti: The well-known law book or code book called *Swsayam-bhuva* is attributed to the great Hindu law-giver, Manu, who lived nearly thirty million years ago. Classified as *Manu-smriti*, it is a collection or digest of current laws which constitute the foundation for Hindu law, and is held in high reverence. The work belongs to a period later than that of the *Vedas*, and is apparently anterior to the philosophical schools. *Manu-smriti* is supposed to have been created before the fifth century B.C. and contains many social and legal records of old Hindu society. Initially it contained 100,000 verses in 24 chapters but later Narada abridged the work into 12,000 verses. Subsequently, it was further shortened to 4,000 verses.

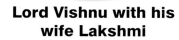

Lord Vishnu with his wife Lakshmi

Bhagvad-gita (philosophy of Life)

This song of the Divine actually constitutes a part of the *World's largest epic Mahabharata.* but is usually referred to separately. It was probably written before second century B.C. and contains some of the most brilliant teachings on the philosophy of life and nature of God to be ever written. A popular chapter in the *Mahabharata* is where Lord Krishna expounds to Arjuna his philosophical doctrines.

Lord Krishna is a manifestation of Vishnu but in this song, he is held to be the Supreme-being. As he was related both to Pandavas and Kauravas who were sons of king Dhritrashtra and Pandu who fought the great war of *Mahabharata*, Lord Krishna refused to take up arms for either side. But he consented to act as Arjuna's (Pandava's brave brother) charioteer. When the two sides confronted each other, Arjuna fearing the imminent slaughter of friends and relations, appealed to Krishna for guidance. It was at this juncture that Krishna began to teach Arjuna about the nature of self, about the path to reach Brahma, about *dharma*, *moksha*, and the doctrine of *bhakti* (faith), etc. In other words, Krishna told Arjuna to do his duty as a soldier without worrying about the consequences. In the second part of the *Mahabharata*, Krishna admitted to being the beholder of the great universal spirit which pervades and constitutes the Universe.

The language of the text is Sanskrit in beautiful verse form and its tone and sentiments are of a lofty character. It is perhaps the only truly philosophical poem in the whole range of literature ever known.

Arjuna is convinced by Lord Krishna's arguments and the battle continues with the Pandavas emerging victorious over their opponents.

Lord Krishna preaching Arjuna during the great war: Mahabharata

Ramayana (Adventures of Lord Rama)

Another great epic of the Hindus is the *Ramayana*---perhaps the oldest of the Sanskrit epics, written by the sage, Valmiki. Composed probably before fifth century B.C., the *Ramayana* gives an account of the life and exploits of Lord Rama. It begins with King Dasharathq becoming father of four sons, the eldest being Rama. Then follow Rama's exile into the forests with his wife Sita and brother Lakshmana; Sita's abduction by Ravana (demon-king of Lanka); the war between Lord Rama and Ravana, ending with the destruction of the demon-king and the rescue of Sita. The story continues with restoration of Rama to the throne of Ayodhya,; the banishment of Sita; her taking up residence in the hermitage of sage Valmiki; the birth of her twin sons Kush and Luv; Rama's discovery and recognition of his children. The story ends with recall of Sita tothe kingdom; the attestation of her innocence; her death; Rama's resolution to follow her before his transition to heaven.

The *Ramayana* is divided into seven *kandas* (chapters) and contains about 50,000 verses. Another version of *Ramayana* was later written by Tulsidas, a devotee of Lord Rama. *Ramayana* is held in high reverence by all Hindus as it gives a picture of the religious, social and political life of ancient India. Even Mahatma Gandhi regarded it as the greatest book on devotional literature.

A verse in this great epic says, "He who reads and repeats this holy life-giving *Ramayana* is liberated from all his sins and exalted with his posterity to the highest heaven." In another chapter, it reads: "As long as the mountains and rivers shall continue on the surface of the earth, so long shall the story of the *Ramayana* be popular in the world."

Lord Rama with Sita Lakshmana and Hanuman

Mahabharata (The Great War)

The *Mahabharata* is the world's longest poem, which continues into about 220,000 lines and dates back to about the ninthcentury B.C. The word 'Mahabharata' refers to a great war fought for supremacy between the Pandavas and the Kauravas.

There was a King named Shantanu who was a descendant of Bharata name. He had a son called Bhishma, who adopted and brought up two of the brothers, Dhritrashtra and Pandu. The younger brother Pandu became the King, but due to a curse he retired to the forest while Dhritrashtra replaced him.

Pandu had five sons known as *Pandavas,* who were noble and good; they represented D*harma* in life. Dhritrashtra had a hundred sons called *Kauravas* and they represented evil and meanness. The theme of the story is the power struggle between *Dharma* and evil, with episodes of love, war, intrigue, morality and immorality interspersed in the text. The events are such as to convey moral, social, political and religious teachings to one and all.

Mahabharata, the Great War between Kauravas and Pandavas

Leading Hindu Gods and Goddesses

The Hindu religion believes in various gods and goddesses, and tells its followers to worship God according to their own faith or *dharma*. It is very liberal in its approach and is tolerant of all other religions. In Hinduism there are several sects, and every sect believes in its own God. Given below are some of the most popular gods worshipped by the Hindus.

Brahma: The four heads of Brahma depict the four cardinal directions of the earth; the four arms refer to the four *Vedas* and are always raised in blessing. Brahma is also the first of the Trinity (the two others being Vishnu the 'preserver', and Mahesh or Shiva, the 'destroyer') and is regarded as the creator of the Universe. He rides on a swan, sitting over a lotus flower. His wife Saraswati is considered the 'goddess of knowledge'.

Vishnu: As the second in Trinity, Vishnu is known as the preserver of the universe. He symbolizes the power of cohesion within the supreme consciousness. He is responsible for preserving fine feelings and is the deity of all householders. Followers of Vishnu are known as *Vaishnavas*. Vishnu reclines on a serpent floating over water, with a lotus arising from his navel. There are twenty-four *avatars* (forms) of Vishnu, some of whom are associated with certain temples and shrines. In his next incarnation, Vishnu, as Lord Kirshna, narrates the philosophy of life as cited in the *Bhagvad Gita*. In South India, Vishnu is known as **Lord Venkateshwara** and a famous temple is dedicated to him at Tirupati.

BRAHMA

VISHNU

Shiva: Lord Shiva is the most energetic God, endowed with a very rich and versatile character in whom can be seen many aspects of human nature. He is also famous as **Nataraja** or the 'joyful lord of dance' and as a fiery destroyer of demons. He was father of Ganesha, married to Goddess Parvati. He is also known as **Mahadeva** or **Mahesh**, besides several other names. As the third in Trinity, he is known as the 'destroyer' of the world. In other words, it means that all that has been created must get destroyed some time or the other.

Krishna: As the eighth incarnation of Vishnu, Krishna represents that unfettered spontaneity of life, which is manifested in love. He is specially popular in northern India, as he is supposed to have lived at *Vrindaban*, near the city of Mathura. He was considered an embodiment of love when young; his captivating beauty had the power to entice young girls. During the great war of *Mahabharata*, he appointed himself charioteer of Arjuna, the warrior. When Krishna found him in a state of confusion, he taught Arjuna the philosophy of life, and this forms the essence of *Bhagvad Gita*.

Rama: The hero of epic *Ramayana* holds a high name in Indian mythology. Rama is also known as *'Purushottam Ram'* which means 'the best of human beings'. Rama was an ideal son who obeyed the dictates of his father by going into exile for fourteen years; an ideal brother who gave full respect to his brother; and an ideal King who sacrificed his all for the good and well-being of his people.

Ganesha: As a Hindu elephant-god, Ganesh is known as lord of wisdom and has been described in detail in another chapter in this book.

SHIVA

KRISHNA

RAMA

Hanuman: As a devotee of Lord Rama, Hanuman occupies a prominent place in mythology and so is worshipped by a large Hindu population, specially on every Tuesday. During Rama's exile in the forest, Hanuman rendered every possible help to Rama and that is why he is considered very compassionate and kind. He is known as *Sankat-mochan* (remover of difficulties), *Bajrangbali* (strong) and *Pavan putra* (son of the wind).

Lakshmi: As goddess of wealth and beauty, Lakshmi is pre-eminently the consort of Vishnu. She is one of the fourteen gems to have sprung up when the gods churned the ocean of milk to procure the nectar of immorality. She is believed to bring fortune and is worshipped especially during the festival of Deepavali.

HANUMAN

Saraswati: As goddess of knowledge and learning, Saraswati represents the organising power of intelligence. She is considered the deity of speech, learning and the arts. She is mostly portrayed as playing the stringed *veena* from which arose the notes in Sanskrit and these happened to be the basis for several modern languages.

SARASWATI, LAKSHMI, GANESH

Durga: This warrior-goddess is depicted as riding a tiger and holding a weapon in each of her ten hands. She is also known as *Mata Vaishno Devi*, and has a shrine in the hills of Jammu region of Kashmir state where she is held in high esteem. Thousands of people throng this shrine in the hope of getting their wishes fulfilled.

DURGA

Prominent Hindu Festivals and Fairs

The Hindus celebrate hundreds of festivals, and most of them have cultural significance and spiritual meanings behind them. The festivals are usually a complex combination of religious ceremonies involving rituals, worship, lustrations, processions, music, dance and feeding of the poor. Many festivals are seasonal: some celebrate the harvest (fertility of the fields), some commemorate the birthday of one or the other God. They have historical significance too as they are intended to purify, to avert malicious influences, to re-energise society, and to stimulate or resuscitate Nature (prayer to rain-God during drought for example). It is difficult to include all the fairs and festivals in this book, but some information about important festivals follows below:

Maha Shivaratri or the great night of Lord Shiva (January-February) is celebrated every month on the eve of the new moon, when the devotees fast all day and late at night worship Lord Shiva. This annual festival is called *Maha Shivaratri* and is held in the Hindu month of *Magha* to commemorate the birth of Lord Shiva.

Vasant Panchami (January-February) is a spring festival marking the first day of spring (*vasant*). All the trees, shrubs and plants bloom with flowers in full glory. People wear yellow clothes and colour their food with saffron to symbolise the ripening of the spring crop. *Saraswati* or goddess of learning is worshipped by the devout. It is a popular festival of Bengal. Hindus, Muslims, Sikhs and Christians fly kites on this day, especially in northern India, where the sky becomes overcast with kites flying everywhere.

Holi - Festival of colours: (February-March) is one of the most colourful Hindu festivals which signifies end of winters and beginning of summers in India. There are different legends related to this festival in Hindu mythology. One such legend says that King Hiranyakashipu was so proud that he declared himself as God, but his own son Prahlad defied. It angered the king and he decided to kill him. His sister Holika had the blessings of never to be burnt by fire. A bonfire was lit with Prahlad to sit in Holika's lap, but it was Holika who was burnt to ashes, while Prahlad remained unhurt. Festival of Holi is considered as victory of good over evil. It is also related to Lord Krishna, and is celebrated with great enthusiasm in Vrindaban and Mathura, the birth place of Lord Krishna. The festival concludes with a midnight bonfire.

Holi : Festival of colours

Ramanaumi (March-April) marks the birthday of Lord Rama, who is considered seventh incarnation of Vishnu. Observed in the month of *Chaitra*), *Ramanaumi* is celebrated by narrating tales from the *Ramayana* and by worshipping Rama. Large quantities of food are distributed to the poor.

Lord Rama

Nag Panchami the snake festival (July-August) is observed on the fifth day of the Hindu month *Shravan* (July-August) to commemorate the victorious return of Krishna after overpowering the serpent Kaliya. People keep fast on this day and bathe on the banks of holy rivers. Some people even believe that poison from the snakes can cure certain diseases on this day. The *nag* (snake) is considered demi-god and malevolent and is worshipped for the sake of warding off evil.

Rakhi or Raksha Bandhan (July-August) is observed on the full moon day of the Hindu month *Shravan*. The festival is celebrated by Hindu and Sikh women and involves tying of the rakhi or an ornamental cord around the wrist of their brothers or other male relatives.. Also called Raksha Bandhan, the festival is celebrated as a

**Rakhi :
an ornamental cord**

commitment by the brother to safeguard his sister/s from all kinds of evil. The threads are usually dyed in yellow or red colour and often a variety of coloured threads ornamented with tassels are used to suit individual tastes. *Tilak* (red vermillion) is applied on the forehead of the brother and a piece of sweetmeat popped into his mouth. In return the brother gives her some gift in cash or kind.

Janamashtami or birthday of Lord Krishna (August-September) is commemorated on the 8th day of the Hindu month *Shravan*. The day preceding Janamashtami is observed with a fast which concludes at midnight, the time when Lord Krishna is said to be born. In Vrindaban, (birthplace of Lord Krishna) and some other parts of northern India the festival is celebrated with great splendour--- temples are decorated with lights and flowers; special fairs are held; and people throng temples till late midnight.

**Krishna
in his child-hood**

Ganesha Chaturthi or Vinayak Chaturthi (August-September) is a festival held to celebrate the birthday of Ganesha or the elephant-God. As Ganesha is the son of Shiva and Parvati, he is worshipped by all Hindus, as is believed to bestow good fortune and remove all obstacles and difficulties in one's path. He is thus worshipped before commencing every important undertaking. The feast is held on the fourth day of the

Hindu month *Bhadrapada* with clay figures of Lord Ganesha worshipped for as many as ten days. At the end of the festival, the idol is immersed in the river or sea and allowed to sink. Ganesha Chaturthi is especially popular in western and central India. It is considered unlucky to see the moon on this day because a curse is said to have been laid on the moon by Lord Ganesha as the former once laughed at him when Ganesha fell off his chariot, the mouse. The moon is said to have craved pardon for having disturbed the equanimity of this son of Lord Shiva.

Festival of Ganesh-Chaturthi

Dussehra or Durga Puja or Navaratra (September-October) is observed during the first half of the month *Ashvin* (September-October). This festival lasts ten days and the tenth day it is called *Vijayadashmi* (the victorious tenth day). It is celebrated all over India, particularly in West Bengal to commemorate the victory of Goddess Durga or Kali, wife of Lord Shiva, over a buffalo-headed demon. The image of Durga is worshipped daily and at the end of the festival, it is immersed into a river. Dussehra is celebrated in north India to commemorate the victory of Lord Rama over demon-king Ravana, known as the victory of good over evil. During this festival alms are distributed freely and musicians go around the streets playing and singing on their instruments.

Dussehra

Diwali/Deepavali : festival of lamps (October-November) is the leading most Hindu festival, observed on the last two days of the dark fortnight. In many parts of India, it is a celebration on return of Lord Rama from exile to his kingdom Ayodhya. To some Hindus the festival signifies the victory of D*harma* (righteousness) and *Ahimsa* (non-violence) over injustice and violence. The festival also commemorates the birth of Goddess Lakshmi, wife of Lord Vishnu and goddess of wealth and fortune.

Lasting for five days in some communities, the first day of Diwali/Deepavali is dedicated to Goddess Lakshmi and windows are kept open to welcome her entry or of wealth into their homes. Many business people close their accounts on this day. Some Hindus keep piles of coins on their ledgers and top the coins with an image of Goddess Lakshmi.

Deepavali

Some people spend their time in gambling. On this day Goddess Lakshmi is worshipped in the evening after a day-long fast. In Bengal, Goddess Kali is the object of worship. The last day is the Deepavali night, when small earthen lamps filled with oil are lighted and placed in rows inside and outside the house. The next day is the beginning of King Vikramaditya era when the said King ascended the throne. It is celebrated by the business community as the New Year.

Bhai-dooj or Bhratridvitya takes place on the third day after *Kali Puja* or *Diwali*. In this festival, sisters in front of their brothers and after lighting the lamp, smear their brothers' foreheads with white sandal paste or rice. They do it with the little finger of their left hand and pray for a happy and prosperous life of their brothers. In return, brothers pray for their welfare and happy life; and also give gifts in cash or kind. The theme of the festival is love, affection and respect for each other.

Kumbh Mela (A fair of earthern pots) is the largest religious fair in India. During some astrological combinations, pots of grain were brought and dipped into the river and then sown along with other seeds to ensure a good harvest. According to a story in the *Vishnu Purana*, when the gods and demons churned the ocean, a vessel full of amrita (nectar of immortality) came out of the ocean. The demons while decamping with the vessel spilled nectar at four places (Allahabad, Haridwar, Ujjain and Nasik in northern and western India). The four cities are sanctified to organise Kumbh Mela every six years in turn.

The biggest such fair falls every twelve years when the sun enters Aries and Jupiter is in Aquarius. The most auspicious place for this fair is Allahabad which is situated at the confluence of the Ganges, Yamuna and Saraswati rivers. A pilgrimage to the Kumbha Mela is regarded as very auspicious, and millions of Hindus and ascetics go to bathe in the holy waters and offer prayers. Many

**Kumbh mela :
wandering Sadhus (holy men)**

people bathe and distribute alms to holy men and mendicants. People believe that a dip in the holy river would wash away all their and their ancestors' sins. Even a great conference of Hindus is held during this fair, where learned metaphysical discussions take place. Naked *sadhus* (saints) lead a big procession and many believe that the mere sight of *sadhus* cleanses them of all their sins.

Eminent Hindu Saints

Veda-Vyasa (3500 B.C.) : The arranger of the Vedas; from the imperishable nature of his work, is also called *shaswata* (immortal). He is the compiler of the four *Vedas*.

Shankaracharya (A.D.788-838): Nambudri Brahmin, Vedantic philosopher and native of Malabar (Kerala). He was a *Saivite* believer in Lord Shiva and established the *Advaita* school of philosophy. His main contribution to Hindu thought was his insistence on the oneness and unity of God. He received the *Vedas* as a divine revelation.

Veda-Vyasa

Vallabhacharya (1479-1531): Son of a Telugu Brahmin; at the age of seven he learnt the four *Vedas*, the six systems of philosophy, and the eighteen *Puranas*. He founded the *Vallabha* sect; his philosophy is based entirely on *bhakti* (devotion) and total surrender to God. His supreme deity is Lord Krishna, the creator of the world.

Vallabhacharya

Chaitanya (1485-1534): Founder of Vaishnava sect which became popular all over India. He was the tenth child of a Brahmin couple of Nadia, Bengal. When twenty-years old he made a trip to Gaya where he turned to the service of Krishna at the behest of a Madhava saint. According to Chaitanya, Krishna was the source, support and end of the world and all other deities Vishnu, Shiva, Narayan and the rest were manifestations of Krishna only. He claimed that faith and devotion to Krishna was more efficacious than knowledge, meditation, charity or virtue. He insisted on the importance of singing and dancing as aid to ecstatic communion between the soul and deity. His favourite form of worship was *kirtan* (choral singing) with the chanting of 'Hare Krishna' in processional worship on the streets of the towns.

Chaitanya

Mira Bai (1450-1547): Hindi poetess and mystic; a Rajput princess of Chittor who married the Rana (prince) of Udaipur; devoted her life to Lord Krishna and became the disciple of saint Raidas. She composed and sang hymns in praise of Krishna. She wrote mostly in the Brij dialect of Hindi. Her last days in Vrindavan (Mathura) were spent in worshipping the image of Krishna with such fervour that the idol came to life and ordered her to follow his path. A fissure arose in the earth and Mira Bai and her Lord disappeared into it.

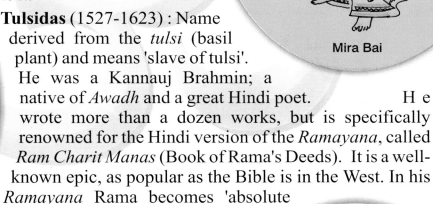

Mira Bai

Tulsidas (1527-1623) : Name derived from the *tulsi* (basil plant) and means 'slave of tulsi'. He was a Kannauj Brahmin; a native of *Awadh* and a great Hindi poet. H e wrote more than a dozen works, but is specifically renowned for the Hindi version of the *Ramayana*, called *Ram Charit Manas* (Book of Rama's Deeds). It is a well-known epic, as popular as the Bible is in the West. In his *Ramayana* Rama becomes 'absolute knowledge and absolute love, symbolising devotion to family and mankind.

Tulsidas

Tukaram (1607-1549): Born near Pune (Maharashtra) in a s*hudra* (low-caste) family; initiated into mysticism by a saint seen in his dream. Most of his hymns are devoted to Krishna. His generosity was boundless and he gave away money and all his possessions to beggars and mendicants.

Vivekananda (1863-1902): Original name Narendranath Dutt; born in Calcutta in a *Kayastha* family; member of the *Brahmo Samaj* (Society of God); disciple of Ramakrishna Paramhans who gave him the new name of Vivekananda that earned him

Tukaram

international fame. In 1893, he participated in the Parliament of Religions where he presented an extremely idealised version of Hinduism. For this he was declared as the wisest man from the East. American newspapers declared him 'an orator by divine right and undoubtedly the greatest figure in the Parliament of Religions. He accepted all faiths as true, but declared that Hindusim was the mother of all religions. He felt that all forms of doubt, disbelief, scepticism, agnosticism and even atheism had a place within the Hindu fold, along with *Vedanta* and *bhakti* (devotion). He defended idolatry and maintained that there was no polytheism in Hinduism, since there was universal acceptance of the one divine power (one God) behind all manifestations. He opposed child marriage and oppression of the lower castes.   He stressed on the need for

Swami Vivekanand

service to the poor, the illiterate and the sick; he believed that no law or religion was higher than 'service to mankind'. He considered Krishna, Buddha, Christ and Ramakrishna as incarnations of one God and declared that he wanted to set up a European forum to promote Indian religions. The Ramakrishna Mission now has over one hundred centres in all parts of the world and is engaged in cultural, educational, social and spiritual activities.

Swami Dayanand Saraswati (1824-1883): A great Hindu social reformer and founder of *Arya Samaj* sect. He fought against the evils of society and struggled to remove untouchability and oppression of low castes (which had become a great evil and divisive force in Hindu society). He pleaded for widow remarriage; was against idol-worship among the Hindus; and in his book *Satyartha Prakash,* he critically examined and compared various religions.

Swami
Dayanand Saraswati

Hindu Wedding

A Hindu wedding is a unique ceremony conducted with recitation of Sanskrit *mantras* (hymns) for each ritual performed. In a conventional marriage ceremony, Sanskrit hymns are recited, which are beyond the comprehension of the modern bride and groom. Hence, many priests usually explain the meanings of the mantras in Hindi or English. The bride and the groom repeat the mantras as directed by the priest, who leads them through the various stages of the ceremony.

- The bride's parents offer *puja* (worship) to their deities and to God Ganesha.

- The bride's parents receive the groom's parents with the marriage party at their house or in a *mandap* (pavilion). The bride arrives from inside the home and exchange garlands with the groom, to the chanting of mantras by the priest.

- The marriage ceremony is held in the *mandap*. The bride is given away by her parents, and the groom promises to take care of the bride as directed by his *dharma* (righteousness).

- Verses conveying their blessings are sung by the members of two parties and the couple are showered with rice grains and flowers at the end of each verse.

- The groom ties the *mangalsutra* (a necklace of black beads) around his bride's neck. The *mangalsutra* is a symbol of marriage.

- The groom takes the bride's right hand and says, "I take your hand, my bride, for good luck. May we grow old together. The Gods have entrusted you to me as my life partner..."

The marriage ceremony is performed before a fire pit, into which the bride and groom make offerings of wood, ghee (clarified butter), grain and roasted millet with prayers to *agni* (fire). They walk around the fire, praying for good luck, health, children and a long and happy married life.

Saptpadi – (seven steps) are taken by the bride and groom by walking together in a line around the holy fire. These seven steps are believed to ensure strength, prosperity, happiness, children, seasonal pleasures and lifelong companionship for the two newly weds.

The priest and senior members of both the families bless the couple. In most cases, all these rituals are completed at night. After conclusion of the ceremonies, the bride is formally taken away to the groom's house.

Traditional Hindu Wedding

HINDU POPULATION IN THE WORLD

The Hindu community is the third largest in the world with over 950 million people living in India. Nepal and other parts of the world.

Top Sixteen Countries with the Largest Hindu Population*

COUNTRY	PERCENT	NUMBER
India	79%	881,000,000
Nepal	89%	18,380,000
Bangladesh	11%	12,630,000
Indonesia	205%	4,000,000
Sri Lanka	15%	2,800,000
Pakistan	1.5%	2,120,000
Malaysia	6%	1,400,000
USA	0.2%	910,000
Mauritius	52%	570,000
South Africa	15%	420,000
United Kingdom	1%	410,000
Guyana	40%	300,000
Fiji	38%	300,000
Surinam	30%	116,000
Bhutan	25%	400,000
Trinidad and Tobago	24%	300,000

As per available data, Hindus are settled in almost every country of the world.